by Nikki Grimes

illustrated by Terry Widener

Shoe Magic

Orchard Books • New York

Contents

The Shoe Rack   5

Tap Shoes   6

Cleats   8

When Devin and Dina Go Hiking   10

Talisha's Toe Shoes   12

Soft Soles   14

Ski Crazy   15

Aaron's Flippers   16

Brandi's Baby Shoes   18

Hockey=Joy   19

Salena's Sandals   21

Running Shoes   22

Golf Shoes for Lu and Yu   24

Work Boots   27

Here Come the Clowns   29

Slippers   30

The Shoe Rack

The shoe rack
Is stacked
With promise,

What you do,

With dreams   Where you go,   Up to be
Waiting   Who you grow   Depends on
To wake.   The steps you take.

Tap Shoes

When music starts playing
Marc hops to his feet.
His soles are slaphappy
His heels stomp the beat
His heart starts a-thumping
His hot blood is pumping
His steel toes are drumming—
Tell Broadway he's coming!
Make way for the new
Tap
    Dance
        King.

Cleats

I'm gonna be
A running back someday.
My brother says no way.
But my cleats don't care
If the socks I wear
Are fuchsia
And my real name is
Clarice.
When I head for the goal line
I'm Rocket,
And all anybody can see
Is the dusty after-trail
Where my feet
Used to be.

When Devin and Dina Go Hiking

Our hiking boots
Are hardly scuffed.
"You'll hike," Mom says,
"When you're old enough."

But wait till we
Are on our own.
We'll climb a mountain.
We'll go alone.

10

We'll dine on berries,
Sip morning dew.
We'll tempt a doe
Out into view.

We'll rest awhile,
Bathe in a brook,
Scout out a cave,
And brave a look.

Before it's dark,
We'll scale the peak,
Ring God's doorbell,
And stay a week.

Then we'll go home,
Though not to stay.
We'll hike for a living—
Does that job pay?

Talisha's Toe Shoes

Your tattered pink
Tricks those who think
You're too frail to hold form.
They scowl at me,
Determining
That I don't fit the norm.

But once we're by
The ankles bound,
We lift on boxy-toes.
Then, proving that
We're tough-enough,
We strike a stubborn pose.

Someday I'll dance
The Nutcracker
(My dream too long deferred).
My arabesque
Will be so fine
They'll redefine the word.

Soft Soles

You walk like a whisper
'Long the hospital hall,
Tell patients you pass
Not to worry at all.

You rush to your ward
On cushions of white
To smooth and fluff pillows,
Set everything right.

You bathe fevered foreheads,
Give needles with care,
And chat with those patients
Who've no family there.

Truck drivers are cool,
And firemen aren't bad,
But Kyle plans on being
A nurse like his dad.

14

Ski Crazy

Standing still,
I feel the cold kiss
Of snow on my cheeks,
The whip of wind
Slashing by.

I bend my knees,
Hear a quiet crunch
Beneath my skis,
And *whoosh!*

I slice
The sugarcoated hillside
In a blink or two,
Slowing only long enough
To seize the view.

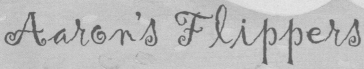

Aaron's Flippers

Air bubbles
And smiling eyes
Are all the conversation
I can offer now.
But someday
We'll talk Dolphinese
Nose to nose.
Though I suppose
You'd rather
Chase sea horses,
Play hide-and-seek
Among the coral,
Or compare the size
Of our flippers.
Have it your way.
But forget rolling over
Or making waves
'Cause I can't compete.
You've already got me beat
Fins down.

Brandi's Baby Shoes

Why Mom keeps
My bronze baby shoes
Buffed and brilliant
On the mantel
Is a mystery.
But lately
I've been thinking:

1.
Maybe Mom set
My shoes in metal
So I'd know
Baby days were over
And I might as well grow.

And

2.
Lucky for the rest of me
She ran out of bronze.

Hockey—Joy

Joy carves the ice.
She shows no fear.
She grips the stick.
Her mind is clear.

She eyes the goal.
She's got the puck.
She knows that goalie's
Out of luck.

"Watch this!" Joy taunts.
She shoots! She—*oops!*
Oh dear. "Sorry, Dad.
Is that a tear?"

Salena's Sandals

March teases me
With spring,
Dishing up
A day of sun,
Memories
Of warmth and fun:
Summer picnics
At the beach,
Dragonflies
In easy reach,
Cruising town
In sandaled feet,
Slurping ice cream
Cool and sweet.
Fireworks,
Water fights,
Humid days,
Muggy nights.
Then I recall—
Spring's just a tease.

And cover my toes
Before they freeze.

Running Shoes

Olympic dreams
Sing me to sleep at night,
And the very sight
Of fancy running shoes
Gets me thinking:
Man! With shoes like those
I wouldn't run—I'd fly.
But my poor pockets
Are only lined with lint.
I could take the hint,
Give up my dreaming.
But words from Daddy
Once whispered in secret
Send my doubts
Into hasty retreat:
"It's not the shoes
That do the runnin'.
It's the feet."

Golf Shoes
for Lu
and Yu

Let's you and me
Survey the green
Like sharp-eyed golfers
We have seen.

You mind my clubs,
Add up the score
'Cause you're my caddie.
(What're best friends for?)

I'll plan my stroke,
Size up the tee—
"The Grand-Slam Kid"
They'll label me.

I'll plant my feet,
Grip the sod,
Select my iron,
And wink at God.

I'll swing and—*pop!*
A hole in one!
Next we'll trade places.
Won't that be fun?

We'll be the best
Kid golfers yet.
No jock will tease us
Then, I bet!

Work Boots

Blayke's boots
Carry him out back
To toolbox
And workbench.
Their sturdy weight
Helps him stand square
While he wields
Hammer and wrench.
The toes are scuffed
The way Blayke likes them,
And they're both
A bit smudged
And weary
After a hard day
At play.
Still, his boots
Hold him steady
Once he's ready
To fix
The world.

Here Come the Clowns

I've got floppy shoes, wax teeth,
And a silly nose that squeaks.
Plus with Mommy's pot of rouge,
I've got bright vermilion cheeks.

Now, when out-of-towners visit,
I put on a five-star show.

I perform my favorite tricks:
Make my nose appear to grow,
Draw a flower from a hat,
Pull a quarter from my ear.

They applaud, and I get tingles.
Boy! I love it when they cheer.

Soon it's time to go to bed.
I bow twice and say good night
Before shuffling up the stairs.
(Mommy says I'm quite a sight.)

I return my nose and teeth
To their box inside my drawer,

Then I scrub my ruddy cheeks
Till they're not red anymore.
Next the size 12 shoes come off.
Once they're neatly put away,

I curl up in bed imagining
The clown I'll be someday.

Slippers

Rest your soles.
Spread your toes.
Curl, breathe deep.
There now, Dreamer,
Hush. . . .
        Sleep.

For Lee Bennett Hopkins. A poet never had a better friend.
—N.G.

To Kate, Kellee, and Michael—wear your shoes well.
—T.W.

Orchard Books, A Grolier Company
95 Madison Avenue, New York, NY 10016

Manufactured in the United States of America
Printed and bound by Phoenix Color Corp. Book design by Nancy Goldenberg
The text of this book is set in 14 point Meridien.
ARTIST'S NOTE: The art was created with Golden acrylics on Strathmore bristol board. First I transfer my sketches onto the bristol board. Then I paint in many thin layers of color to give the art a "glow" and a transparent quality.—T.W.

1 3 5 7 9 10 8 6 4 2

Library of Congress Cataloging-in-Publication Data
Grimes, Nikki.
Shoe magic / by Nikki Grimes ; illustrations by Terry Widener.—lst ed.
p. cm.
Summary: Poems describe the different shoes children wear—including sandals, running shoes, golf shoes, and work boots—and the career dreams that go with them.
ISBN 0-531-30286-5 (alk. paper)—ISBN 0-531-33286-1 (lib. bdg.)
1. Shoes—Juvenile poetry. 2. Children's poetry, American. 3. Careers—Juvenile poetry. [l. Shoes—Poetry.
2. American poetry. 3. Careers—Poetry.] I. Widener, Terry, ill. II. Title.
PS3557.R489982   S48   2000   811'.54—dc21   99-24898